A
Cottage
Garden
Alphabet

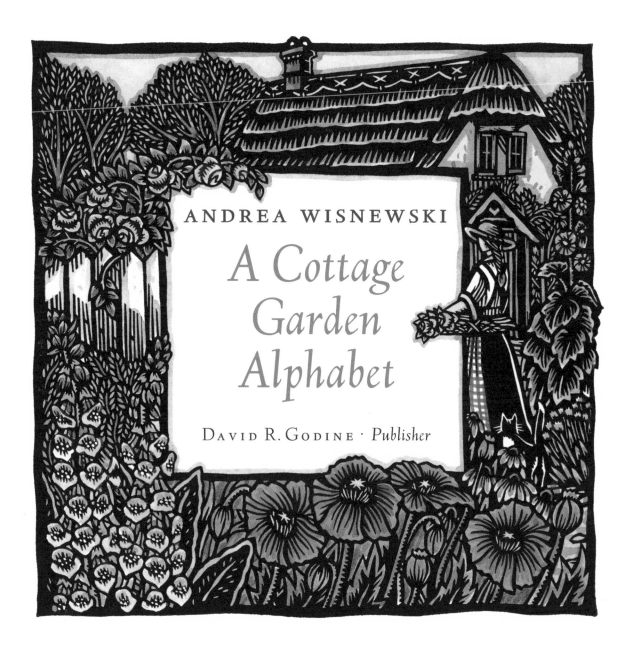

ANDREA WISNEWSKI

A Cottage Garden Alphabet

David R. Godine · Publisher

For my mother and father.

I would like to give loving thanks to my husband, Chris Butler,
who always comes to my rescue with his advice and support.
My great appreciation also goes to Elizabeth Moody and Marianne Gourary
for always believing in this book. Also for my daughter, Allison,
who didn't mind her mother constantly coloring.

———————————

First published in 2002 by
David R. Godine, Publisher
Post Office Box 450
Jaffrey, New Hampshire 03452
www.godine.com

LIBRARY OF CONGRESS CATALOGING-IN-PUBLICATION DATA

Wisnewski, Andrea.
A cottage garden alphabet / Andrea Wisnewski.—1st ed.
p.   cm.
ISBN 1—56792—229—5 (alk. paper)
1. Cottage Gardening. 2. Cottage Gardens. 3. Handicraft.
4. English language—Alphabet. I. Title.
SB454.3.C67 W57 2002
635—dc21   2002012879

FIRST EDITION
Printed in Hong Kong

ABCD
EFGHIJ
KLMNO
PQRST
UVWX
Y&Z

MY GARDENING MEMORIES from childhood involve biting insects, hot, scorching sun, and an incident having to do with weeds and seedlings too embarrassing to discuss further. Let's just say I was not a natural-born horticulturist. Although green thumbless I was still drawn to the beauty of the garden. As a child I had a difficult time resisting the temptations that flowers offered, especially picking them. I often came into the house with an offering of contraband flowers gathered from neighbors' gardens for my horrified mother. As I grew and went to find my own bit of earth to tend I found out just how little I knew. Plants are needy little things and — like children — their needs are all different. I can try to be a strict parent, telling them to behave themselves and just grow nicely where they are put but — also like children — they don't listen. They all want special treatment. So you make bargains with them: "I will move you to that prime sunny location and make that hollyhock move over but you'd better bloom this year." This sort of thing can go on all summer if I don't put my foot down early in the season and maintain some sort of control. These problems aside, I enjoy gardening now more than ever. In the planning stage, often during the winter months, I will cover many scraps of paper with my elaborate designs. This book was created along similar lines; during the long winter months and on many, many scraps of paper.

The designs in this book were created in papercut. The papercuts begin as sketches on vellum. When I have tweaked the sketch to my satisfaction the design is transferred onto a black, clay-coated paper. Most of the design's details come out in the cutting process, for which I use a #11 X-acto blade and lots and lots of patience. When a cut is complete, a magnesium plate is made of the design. The plate is then printed on a 32 x 34 press hand-built by my husband Chris. Often the print is hand colored with watercolor. The finished prints have the effect of a woodcut and not the microsurgery with a scalpel that they are.

IS FOR

Arbor

B

IS FOR

Beehive

C

IS FOR

Cottage

D

IS FOR

Daffodil

E

IS FOR

Eggs

F

IS FOR

Foxglove

G

IS FOR

Gardener

H

IS FOR

Hollyhock

I

IS FOR

Iris

J

IS FOR

Johnny
Jump-up

K

IS FOR

Kitchen
Garden

L

IS FOR

Lavender

M

IS FOR

Morning Glory

IS FOR

Nicotiana

O

IS FOR

Orchard

P

IS FOR

Primula

Q

IS FOR

Quince

R

IS FOR

Roses

S

IS FOR

Scarecrow

T

IS FOR

Topiary

U

IS FOR

Urn

IS FOR

Vegetables

W

IS FOR

Watering Can

IS FOR

Xtra

Y

IS FOR

Yarrow

Z

IS FOR

Zucchini

A Cottage Garden Alphabet

has been set in a digital version of Frederic Goudy's Deepdene. Designed in 1927 for the Monotype Corporation, Deepdene bears a distinct family resemblance to the types Goudy designed for hand composition, yet is free of the short descenders that mar most of the types he designed for machine composition. Frankly decorative in their details, both the roman and the italic (like many of Goudy's types) recall his early experience as a designer of letters for advertising and magazines, as well as his abiding interest in the types created at the height of the fine press movement of the late nineteenth and early twentieth centuries. Notable for its spontaneous drawing and strong vertical emphasis, Deepdene is considered one of Goudy's most successful faces. ¶ The display letters are Goudy Handtooled, a robust open face that blends the decorative characteristics of hand-lettering for display with the rhythms of Goudy's text types.

Design by Carl W. Scarbrough